T0129963

CUT OFF
AND
RELAYS

TOMAS GIL

author**HOUSE**

AuthorHouse™
1663 Liberty Drive
Bloomington, IN 47403
www.authorhouse.com
Phone: 1 (800) 839-8640

© 2019 Tomas Gil. All rights reserved.

No part of this book may be reproduced, stored in a retrieval system, or transmitted by any means without the written permission of the author.

Published by AuthorHouse 11/30/2019

ISBN: 978-1-7283-3736-4 (sc)
ISBN: 978-1-7283-3735-7 (e)

Library of Congress Control Number: 2019919554

Print information available on the last page.

Any people depicted in stock imagery provided by Getty Images are models, and such images are being used for illustrative purposes only. Certain stock imagery © Getty Images.

This book is printed on acid-free paper.

Because of the dynamic nature of the Internet, any web addresses or links contained in this book may have changed since publication and may no longer be valid. The views expressed in this work are solely those of the author and do not necessarily reflect the views of the publisher, and the publisher hereby disclaims any responsibility for them.

LETTER TO THE READER

I wrote this booklet because of my concern for what I feel is a great problem in baseball today - the principal essence of the game is missing. The basic fundamentals of the game, those things which make a complete baseball player are not emphasized in baseball today. The lack of the BASICS allows the game to be played in a mediocre fashion. The art of cut-offs and relays requires team work and concentration. It requires complete knowledge of the BASICS and the discipline that goes with doing them over and over.

Having an idea on how these are executed and its continuous practice, not only will make the player a better baseball player, but, will also give him a sense of responsibility. This responsibility will stay with the player for life.

The other reason why I decided to write this booklet is my concern, and that of society, with the problem of drugs and alcohol in sports, in school, in society. I feel I had a very happy childhood. My parents might not have had the needed economic resources, but they where always at my side encouraging my ideals and aspirations. At this time in my life, there are some things which they gave me that have more worth than all the material things they could have given me, and that is, the sense of responsibility, self-respect, and the need to be constant in all that I do.

I had the opportunity of playing professional baseball for nineteen years. I might not have had the physical abilities of many other players, but my desire to make something of myself, made me a useful player - a team player. I was the player that did the things the manager said, I studied the game, and displayed a determination and consistency that allow me to stay in the game for a long time.

For the last few years I have been instructing others about the game of baseball. I have seen many youngsters who have not "made it" and some who have. If we observe the youngsters under our tutelage, they will give us signs as to where they are and if we can help them.

I find it in bad taste to see a Little League coach with beer in hand at the conclusion of a game. If the coaches require from our youngsters some discipline, and demand the best from their game playing, we as coaches should be the first to set an example. I believe that the baseball park is not the best place for alcohol, especially in front of our youngsters.

Twenty six years ago a manager advice me never to leave the locker room with a beer in hand since I never knew when a youngster would come and ask me for an autograph. In order to sign the autograph I would have to give him the beer to hold. This made a great impact on me. I realize that just the wearing of the uniform was a high for me. I did not need the use of alcohol for that. Besides, by using the uniform, I was representing my family, community, state, and in many occasions my country.

The game of professional baseball offers many temptations. It is painful for me to watch how teammates who demonstrated great ability at the game loose the best years of their lives by their abuse of alcohol, and in many cases their use of drugs.

I have always had a strong believe in God and his spiritual force. I believe all human beings should have a higher force to help them deal with all the pressures in life. Whatever an individual believes in - he should be faithful to it and consistent. This believe has kept me in life.

I hope this booklet can project this believe. Baseball has been my life. It has required determination, consistency, loyalty and most of all discipline. But then what else is life.

Gustavo Gil

CHILDREN AND BASEBALL

Children learn about baseball much earlier than when a coach starts with his first practice; he throws with his dad and tries to hit the ball; he runs around the imaginary bases and has fun doing it.

In only a few years, this youngster will be in a Little League team where with community help and in a structured recreational atmosphere he will continue to learn moral and spiritual values, shape his character and improve his physical appearance. Irrelevant of age and where he plays, the goal of all these youngsters is to improve their ability to play and be successful.

As a whole, all teams have their managers and coaches to help these youngsters meet their goals. It is to these "Greats" - managers and coaches - that I dedicate these few lines.

I had the opportunity to listen to a statement made by a very creditable individual that censure the fact that many of the Major League ex-baseball players where not managing or coaching Little League teams.

The experience of a player in a Major League team, does not necessarily make a good manager or coach in Little Leagues. In some instances this player rather than helping, could be hurting these youngsters that are trying to become good baseball players. In reality, a Little League game does not have to be a miniature game of the New York Yankees.

Many of the coaches with experience in Major Leagues are inclined to teach as if they were in Major Leagues, instead of teaching in Little Leagues. It is a mistake to try to make the new players boost themselves to the stature of the teacher, when the correct approach is for the teacher to adjust himself or herself to its pupils.

In the legal baseball field, the bases are at a distance of 90 feet, and it has been like that since 1845 when Alexander Cartwright made the first baseball diamond. If the distance changes between bases, the balance of the game will also change.

In stealing of bases in Major League games, the play is regularly a very close one. In a double play, the play on first base is usually a close play, trying to score from second with a hit to the outfield, the player practically has very little time to score. In a field with the shorter dimensions, the symmetry of the game changes completely, the fast runners would steal the bases with ease, the double plays would become much harder and since the outfielders would have to play closer, the possibilities of scoring from with a hit to second base would be much more difficult.

In many instances the strategy of the game will change, for example, a professional player would be advanced to second base with a sacrifice hit, then try to score from there with a base hit to the outfield, something which you see very seldom in Little Leagues. In Little Leagues the fastest runner is more apt to steal second base; in the Major Leagues it is very rare to see a player trying to steal third base course, no one likes to loose, but when one looses, teach the youngster how to loose - keep his spirits high and teach him how to accept it with grace. This will mold his personality and will guide him on the road to success. Remember that you are not only the team manager but you are also the teacher. You can be assured that your influence can make this young athlete a good citizen in the future.

I believe that more than anything else, the coach needs to be understanding, since he always needs to have in hand a message of encouragement that could give a sense of self-assuredness to that young player who at that particular moment feels things are just not going right. If a manager seriously accepts his responsibilities towards his players, and does not take things personally, he will have done the proper thing.

Feel proud when you see your team playing better each time they compete. This, together with the fact that the youngsters are developing a responsibility and enjoying themselves, will give you a great satisfaction as a manager. It will also make you feel that you are reaching your goals.

All managers should promote a **WINNING SPIRIT**. This spirit is the quality that makes the youngsters play better than what they feel they are capable. This spirit is like a contagious virus. All managers owe this winning spirit to their players, their fans and to the community. In other words, the manager is the direct communicator of this winning spirit.

The manager must possess great courage and self-assurance. He must do what is best for his team, independent of what is said by parents, fans, and of course, those who sit on the bleachers - those that always know <u>what</u> should have been done after the game is over. He must be ready to accept criticisms - some will be constructive and some will not. Your decisions might not be right for some, but, if it was the best for your players, for your team, then you have done your job.

Remember the best trophy that a manager can receive in Little Leagues will not be seen except but with the passing of time - that is when you see that many of the youngsters that were under your guidance have become good and useful citizens.

The game of professional baseball offers many temptations. It is painful for me to watch how teammates who demonstrated great ability at the game loose the best years of their lives by their abuse of alcohol, and in many cases their use of drugs.

I have always had a strong believe in God and his spiritual force. I believe all human beings should have a higher force to help them deal with all the pressures in life. Whatever an individual believes in - he should be faithful to it and consistent. This believe has kept me in life.

I hope this booklet can project this believe. Baseball has been my life. It has required determination, consistency, loyalty and most of all discipline. But then what else is life.

Gustavo Gil

INTRODUCTION TO CUT-OFFS AND RELAYS

This is one of the most important phases within baseball; many players have been born with a running and batting ability, but none of them knowing the movements needed for cut-offs and relays. Each one of the players must know where he must go with or without the ball. If the cut-offs and relays are performed as they should, you would be surprised about how many close games can be won.

You must keep in mind that when you perform a defensive play, there is always someone running against you playing an offensive play. Communication with teammates and not loosing time with defensive movements is extremely important.

GENERAL OBJECTIVES

1. All your throws should chest high, this way the fielders can manage it with ease.
2. If you see that there is no opportunity for an out to the front runner, cut it off and quickly observe if there is an opportunity to make another play for an out. **NEVER THROW THE BALL IF THERE IS NO OPPORTUNITY TO MAKE A PLAY.**
3. Always try to catch the ball from the side where you have the glove and make sure you do it with both hands.
4. Communicate with your teammates, it is very important, the voices should be heard.

5. Be aggressive. Do not worry if your decisions are not right. Because this goes with the process of learning.

6. You must be flexible, if the strategies of the play change, you must react and remember: NOTHING is defined in the area of cut-offs and relays.

7. When you are relaying or cutting-off the ball, throw it from the position from which you have caught it, since you do not have time to position yourself.

8. Make your own decisions, don't depend on what you hear.

9. Don't let the ball go to a base where there is not going to be a play.

10. THINK ON THE GAME OF BASEBALL, CONCENTRATE AND MAINTAIN YOURSELF IN THE GAME.

11. It is of the greatest importance that you know who your teammates are - their reaction in and out of the baseball field.

12. The most important thing is **YOUR PHYSICAL CONDITION -** a balanced diet and keeping your body free of drugs and alcohol.

All the plays discussed in this booklet are defensive plays, in other words, you have to do everything possible to stop the attack from the opposite team.

BASIC RULES FOR EACH POSITION

Outfielders (Communication)

All the throws must chest high, this way the player who does the relay can manage the ball with ease.

Place yourself in a position from which you can throw the ball in the fastest and quickest way. Always behind the ball, so you can accomplish better forward movements when you are fielding.

Field the ball from the side from which you are to throw it. Remember, anyone can field the ball, but the outfielders must be capable of stopping the runners from taking an extra base.

Infielders (Communication)

Assume your position as soon as possible, place your body in a position for cut-off and relay, fielding from the side in which you have the glove; if you have to cut-off the throw and then throw to another base, you must catch the ball from the side from which you throw.

Pitchers (Communication)

Don't get discouraged, don't keep your head down after someone connects with a hit, be the back-up man and always do it as deep as possible against the fence or in front of the dugout.

STRATEGY 1

SITUATION: No man on base - base hit to right field.

STRATEGY: Ball goes from right field to the second baseman who will be the cut-off man.

1st BASE: Stays on first base, makes sure that the runner steps on the base.

2nd BASE: Goes to the shallow right field on line with the base and the ball.

3rd BASE: Backs-up the Short Stop.

SHORT STOP: Covers second base.

PITCHER: Stays on the mound.

Catcher follows runner to 1st base

The enemy must not reach 2nd base. If we maintain our bodies clean and healthy from drugs and alcohol we can contain the enemy - whether on the baseball field or in life.

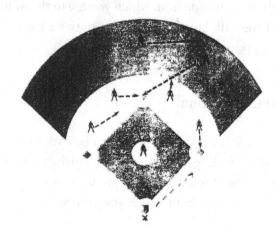

STRATEGY 2

SITUATION: No man on base a base hit to center field.

STRATEGY: The ball goes from CF to Ss or to the 2nd baseman who will be in line with the base, thus containing the runner from going to 2nd base.

1st BASE: Stays on his position and makes sure that the runner steps on the base.

2nd BASE: Moves to shallow center in line with the ball and the base

3rd BASE: Stays on third.

SHORT STOP: Goes to cover second base. If the ball is hit towards the Ss, you make a change, the Ss goes to the position for a cut-off and the second baseman covers the bag.

PITCHER: Stays on the mound.

To keep in line with the ball and the base is as important as it is to maintain a line of respect with our parents and coaches.

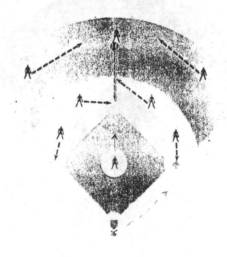

STRATEGY 3

SITUATION: Hit to the left field, no man can base.

STRATEGY: Ball goes from the left fielder to Ss who should be in line with second base.

1ˢᵗ BASE: Back-up to second baseman on the throw from left field.

2ⁿᵈ BASE: Covers second base.

3ʳᵈ BASE: Stays on third.

SHORT STOP: Goes out to the shallow left field in line with second base.

PITCHER: Stays on the mound.

Catcher follows the runner to 1B

If we concentrate on the responsibilities of staying on our positions, we will learn how to be responsible with all our actions.

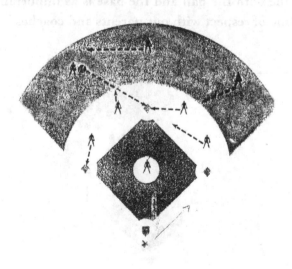

STRATEGY 4

SITUATION: Man on first base, hit to the right field.

STRATEGY: The ball goes from the right field to the third base.

1ˢᵗ BASE: Stays on first base and makes sure that runner steps on base.

2ⁿᵈ BASE: Covers second base.

3ʳᵈ BASE: Stays on third base.

SHORT STOP: Places himself in line with ball and third base in position as a cut-off man.

PITCHER: Positions himself a short distance behind 3ʳᵈ base as a back-up.

In order to exercise any play, one must depend on the team and their ability to play. In life we are part of a team - parents, school, community. Make sure they all know how to play so you can make the right choices.

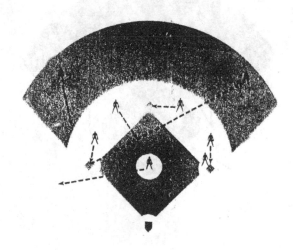

STRATEGY 5	Our fielder back up.
SITUATION:	Man on first, base hit to center field.
STRATEGY:	Ball goes from center fielder to 3rd base.
1st BASE:	Stays on his position.
2nd BASE:	Covers second base.
3rd BASE:	Covers third base.
SHORT STOP:	Places himself in a position in line with ball and third base as a cut-off man.
PITCHER:	Goes at a short distance behind third base bag as a back-off man.

Our enemy, drugs and alcohol, will continue with its pressures and will try to reach us - but we will maintain our positions and use all those around us (parents, school, church and community) to help us.

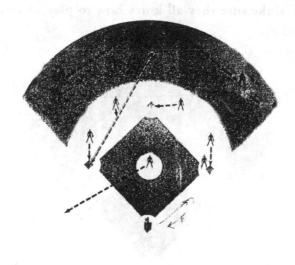

STRATEGY 6	Outfielder.
SITUATION:	Man on first, base hit to left field.
STRATEGY:	Ball goes from the left fielder to the third baseman.
1ˢᵗ BASE:	Stays on his position.
2ⁿᵈ BASE:	Covers second base.
3ʳᵈ BASE:	Covers third base.
SHORT STOP:	Goes to the position of a cut-off man in line with the ball and the 3ʳᵈ base.
PITCHER:	Back-up on third base.

Catcher

The pressures from the outside will continue, but by now we have created a sense on responsibility for ourselves and have maintain our discipline so as to move ahead with our lives.

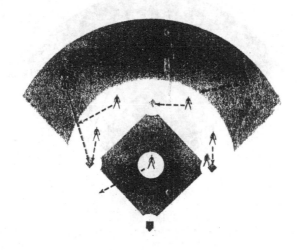

STRATEGY 7

SITUATION: Man on second, base hit to the right field.

STRATEGY: The ball goes from right field to home plate.

1ˢᵗ BASE: He will be the cut-off man in the infield.

2ⁿᵈ BASE: Covers first base.

3ʳᵈ BASE: Covers third base.

SHORT STOP: Covers second base.

PITCHER: Backs - up the catcher behind home plate.

If you break your line of responsibility by using drugs and alcohol, this will affect you at home, school, and in all your activities. You must always be aware, in the right position, in order to protect all those things dear to you.

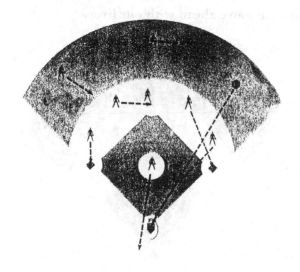

STRATEGY 8

SITUATION:	Man on second, base hit to center field.
STRATEGY:	Ball is thrown from center field to home plate.
1st BASE:	Main cut-off man, places himself on top of the pitchers mound.
2nd BASE:	Covers first base.
3rd BASE:	Covers third base.
SHORT STOP:	Covers second base.
Pitcher:	Backs-up the catcher behind home plate.

We must always be on the alert and say NO to drugs. By saying NO we strengthened our character. If all fails our back-ups will always be there in place to protect us.

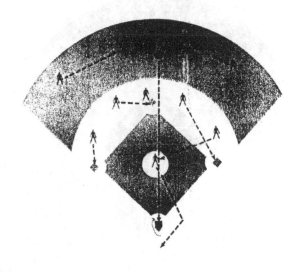

STRATEGY 9

SITUATION: Man on second, base hit to left field.

STRATEGY: Ball goes from the left fielder to home plate.

1ˢᵗ BASE: Stays on first base.

2ⁿᵈ BASE: Covers second base.

3ʳᵈ BASE: Main cut-off man on the infield.

SHORT STOP: Covers third base.

PITCHER: Back-up to the catcher behind home plate.

The pressure to use drugs will continue all around you. You will win. You have developed a straight line with your principles and will not allow drugs to touch you.

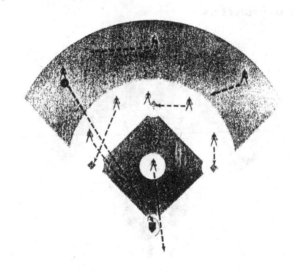

STRATEGY 10

SITUATION: Extra base to the right center field with no man on base.

STRATEGY: The ball goes from right-center to second base and from there to third, in order to hold the runner on second base.

1st BASE: Stays on first and makes sure that runner steps on bag.

2nd BASE: He is the relay man, goes to the shallow right field to relay the ball to third base.

3rd BASE: Covers third base.

SHORT STOP: Goes behind 2nd base and stays at a short distance and lets him know where he should throw.

PITCHER: Backs-up the third base.

At times we feel confuse by the pressures to use drugs and alcohol or by maybe that extra base - maybe a friend started using drugs. Our minds are made up - we will stay in line.

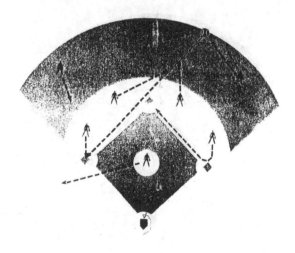

STRATEGY 11

SITUATION: Extra base to left center field with nobody on base.

STRATEGY: The ball goes from the left center to the Ss and from there to third base to hold the runner from reaching third.

1st BASE: Makes sure the runner steps on the bag and when the runner passes, he follows him to 2nd base.

2nd BASE: Back-up for Short Stop and places himself at a short distance and lets him know as to where he should throw.

3rd BASE: Covers third base.

SHORT STOP: Main cut-off man. Goes to the short area of left center to relay the ball to the 3rd base.

PITCHER: Back-up behind third base.

We cannot be weak and we must always be ready for all the pressures that we will encounter - in school, community and sometimes at home.

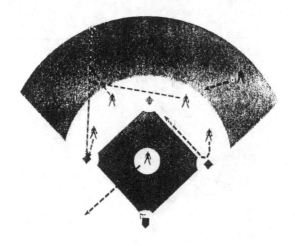

STRATEGY 12

SITUATION: Extra base hit to the right - center with runner on first.

STRATEGY: Ball goes from right - center to the second base were it will be relayed to either third or home plate depending on what the runner will do.

1st BASE: Must be flexible, begins to follow the runner to second base, from there he lines up with second base and home plate.

2nd BASE: Main cut-off man. Goes towards right center to relay the throw from outfield to 3rd base.

3rd BASE: Covers third base.

SHORT STOP: Back-up second base at a short distance.

PITCHER: Comes half way between third and home plate, and from there he goes to back-up where the play is to occur.

If you are surrounded by friends who are clean and sober - all the tricks used will not weaken you - your sense of responsibility for yourself is in line.

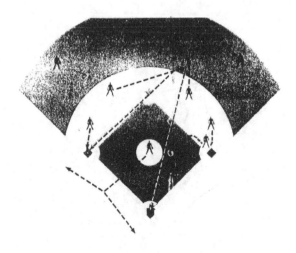

STRATEGY 13

SITUATION: Extra base hit to left-center field with runner on first.

STRATEGY: Ball goes from the left center to Ss who throws to third base or to home (depending on what the runner does).

1st BASE: Must be flexible, begins to follow the runner to second base, from there be places himself as the relay person between Ss and home plate.

2nd BASE: Back-up the Ss and will follow him at a short distance.

3rd BASE: Covers third base.

SHORT STOP: Is the main cut-off man, he goes to the shallow left center to relay to third base or to the home plate.

PITCHERS: Come half-way between third base and home plate with the expectation that from there he will go to were there is a play.

The pressures continue to attack us. This time the strategy changes - all of our team (friends, family, community) is one of responsibility for each other and have a strong moral base - so we do not succumb under pressures. We know what is the right play.

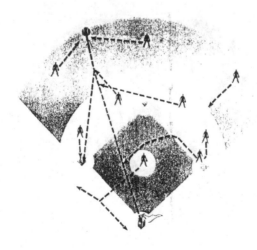

STRATEGY 14

SITUATION: Throwing the ball around the infield after an infield out.

STRATEGY: Do it always, throw the ball the least amount possible; example, from first to second base, from there to the short stop and from the short stop to third base. He in turn will throw the ball to the pitcher. The pitcher should always receive the ball from the third base.

RUNNING THE BALL AFTER A STRIKE OUT:

The team must throw the ball as it best suits them. The only thing is to keep it simple and remember: the ball returns to the pitcher through the third baseman.

BE ORGANIZED AND CONSISTENT.

In life, keep it simple. Be determine, constant and discipline.

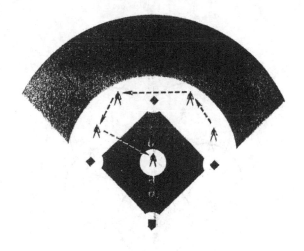

STRATEGY 15

SITUATION: Fly hits to the infield.

STRATEGY: Never ask for the ball with much of anticipation. Wait for till ball reaches its highest level, and remember that the infielder that moves forward has the best chance of making the play.

If a teammate calls for the tall, move out of his way don't argue.

When you go to make the play, move towards the ball and never place yourself directly under it.

Never let the pressure in live change your approach to living. Using common sense, keeping things simple, and being determine and consistent will give you victory. In our private lives you can be productive, respected and admired individuals if you maintain these strategies.

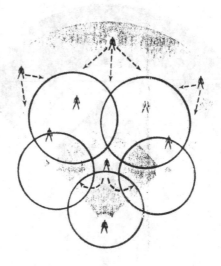

BUNTING

The sacrifice play is an attempt to bunt the ball down, either to the first or third base line in order to move a runner or runners into scoring position.

A good bunt is difficult to defend against, thus it becomes a doubly important offensive play.

It is essential that you attempt to bunt only low pitchers. The high pitch is easily popped up as a fly ball.

Every attempt should be made to force the first baseman to field the bunt with a runner on first, and the third baseman to field the bunt with runners at first and second base.

TIPS

1. Make the first baseman field the bunt with runner at first.
2. Make the third baseman field the bunt with runners at first and second.
3. Don't attempt to bunt a high pitch.
4. Base runners must be sure that the ball has been bunt on the ground before advancing to the next base.

Use the head of the bat to bunt

You must balance your body in order to be ready to bunt no matter how your style of ??? and your body must be ??? and ??? must be ??? in the home plate.

BUNTING STRATEGY 2

SITUATION: Runners on first and second.

STRATEGY:

1st Baseman:	Breaks toward home plate
2nd Baseman:	Covers first base.
3rd Baseman:	Breaks towards home plate, the very second he realizes that he cannot field the ball, he must move quickly to cover third base.
Short Stop:	Covers second base.
Pitcher:	Breaks toward the right side of the mound.
Outfielders:	All break in towards the infield.

Catcher call the play

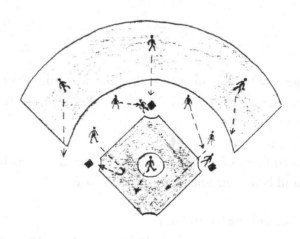

IF YOUR YOUNG ATHLETE.......

1. If your young athlete starts showing signs of being excited for no apparent reason,
2. If your young athlete begins to perspire more that usual,
3. If your young athlete appears distant from the rest of the teammates,
4. If your young athlete appears quieter than usual,
5. If your young athlete is always punctual and then suddenly starts to show up late,
6. If your young athlete start lying to you,
7. If your young athlete begins to leave the game before it is finished,
8. If your young athlete begins to show-up at practice with blood shot eyes,
9. If your young athlete starts showing signs of an accelerated heartbeat,
10. If your young athlete begins to fight with his teammates for no legitimate reason,

Then these are signs that your young athlete might have some type of problem and it might be a good time to try to help him. Remember that as his/her coach or manager you know your players' habits almost as well as the parents.

TO THE PARENTS AND AFICIONADOS

I have accumulated over a period of 25 years in professional baseball and five years as manager in the Minor Leagues a few thoughts I would like to share with you.

Baseball begins in this country at an early age. Parents and aficionados attend the games, practices and many of the activities that occur around the game of baseball.

This is very important, since you can see the desire and interest that the youth display for the game. However, I am worried about the attitude of many parents for their children, which I personally feel is not appropriate.

I believe that some parents expect their children to act as "great" baseball players, when in many cases these kids are just beginning to learn the game. They do it because obviously they enjoy it, but this interest could be lost by the way the parents behave in the baseball field.

Many parents scream at their children, and others want to instruct them during the game. There comes a time when the child, who went to the baseball field to have fun, realizes that it is a torture for him to play the game.

Parents must realize that baseball is a very difficult game. Baseball is a physical game but also a game of instincts. Your children are developing physically and at the same time learning how to adjust, so it is absurd for you to think that a youngster at this early age can assimilitate all the instructions and skills that are being taught. Those of us who chose this discipline as a profession, have taken many years to achieve it, years of practice, sacrifice, and dedication. This is a discipline that has to be practiced daily if one wants to make a name in this field. Yet many of us want our children to act like those people who have dedicated all their lifes to the game of baseball.

Personally, because of my years of experience, I think that these youngsters should be allowed to develop aptitudes in accordance to their physical capacity. If you do this you will see how those who really have the physical qualities and the desire for self-improvement will progress. If a youngster really has the desire to play professional baseball, he will have many years ahead of him to help him perfect not only his ability but the quality of his game.

Baseball for me is a vocation, something that requires practice, needs lots of dedication, and a desire to excel at the game. Of course, not all who practice the game nowadays will become professional baseball players, and this is another factor for my argument - Why all this pressure on these youngsters that begin playing the game for fun?

I have had the opportunity of seeing professional baseball players frustrated, and unable to achieve much, because they signed a baseball contract just to satisfy their parents. This is not only harming the youngster but also the parent who has to live with the frustration of seeing that his son did not become what he wanted.

I had a father who loved baseball. There wasn't a baseball game where I was playing that he would not be there. But I can honestly say that my father never interfered with my game, he never disagreed with the manager, although he did do something that really upset me (today, as a parent myself I see where this is very natural) he would brag about "his son" everytime I made a good play.

It is good that you are concerned, aware and present at the games, but let the children have fun. After all, baseball is a game.

I am also concern about the way some people attack the umpires and team managers. In most cases, it is an injustice, since these men perform this activity because they love baseball, and after all they are part of your children's growth and that discipline they will carry for the rest of their lives. To be a manager in Little Leagues you need a special personality. But there are many parents who go to the baseball games just to criticize these men for their decisions during the game. This same man is the one that spends his time trying to help your youngster, and in the majority of the cases does not receive any monetary gratification for his work.

I have yet to know a player who has become a better player by arguing with the umpire. I played professional baseball for 19 years, this without counting my years as a youth or my amateur years. I was never expelled from the game. Respect is something that not only stays in the baseball field, but you carry it to the streets, home or wherever you may be.

We should learn how to control our emotions. Just as our children go to the baseball field to learn to play the game of baseball, so must we learn how to respect the managers and umpires. After all it is just a game.

WHAT IS MARIJUANA?

MARIJUANA is one of the types of drugs developed from a plant called Cannabis Sativa. Its principal psychoactive ingredient is THC, (Delta 9 Tetrahydrocannabinol). It also contains more than 400 chemical ingredients. The amount of THC determines the effects on the person who eats it or smokes it.

When you smoke marijuana, the THC is absorbed by the majority of the organs and tissues of the body. Marijuana is damaging to the lungs and pulmonary systems. It has been determine that marijuana smoke contains more cancer-causing agents than tobacco.

Many youngsters are introduced to smoking marijuana by their friends; generally schoolmates, brothers or sisters. Peer pressure is a big factor in the beginning use of marijuana. Research has indicated that the earlier an individual begins to use marijuana, the greater the probability that they would experiment with other drugs.

Research has proven that the students do not remember what they have learned while under the influence. The effects of the use of marijuana can interfere with learning since this reduces the ability to perform tasks that require concentration and coordination.

Some of the immediate physical effects of smoking or eating marijuana are the following: a substantial increase in the heart rate, bloodshot eyes, a dry mouth and throat, and increase appetite. Some of the studies indicate that the use of marijuana during pregnancy can result on premature births and low-weight births. It can also influence the hormonal levels related with sexuality. These results can be very detrimental during puberty. Marijuana can also produce paranoia and psychosis.

Other types of Cannabis besides marijuana are: tetrahydrocannabinol, hashish and hashish oil. Marijuana has other names: pot, grass, weed, reefer, dope, Mary Jane, sinsemilla, Acapulco Gold, and Thai sticks. The other types have been called THC, hash, and hash oil.

WHO IS TOUCHED BY THE PROBLEM OF DRUGS AND ALCOHOL?

Do you know someone who is using drugs? Have you seen the consequences of this destructive habit?

Maybe you think that this problem will never touch you or your children. Or, if you are a teacher, hasn't it ever occurred to you that in your own classroom there could be a youngster who has a drug problem or has the potential for such a problem. The issue of drug abuse is a problem for all us, it is your problem, it knocks at your door and mine every day.

As parents, teachers, coaches, responsible members of society, we <u>must</u> educate ourselves about the dangers of drugs. This way we are aware, and we can help our children, family members and friends in convincing them that drugs are morally wrong.

ALCOHOL

Its availability and acceptance by society, makes this one of the most difficult drugs to control. Alcohol is one of the oldest drugs known to man. It is also the main cause of automobile accidents among adolescents.

Alcohol has been known to affect the pancreas, esophagus, stomach, heart and the liver. The Inspector General has stated that pregnant women should not use alcohol during their pregnancy, particularly during the first three months, because of its prejudicial effect on the fetus.

Alcohol can cause individuals to be depressed, thus causing diminished coordination, vision, and reflexes or it can cause emotional reactions such as, hostility, passivity and withdrawal. In cases of excessive use it can be addictive in that the individual needs to increase the dosage to obtain a desired effect. It is a progressive disease and terminal.

INHALANTS

Inhalants are very easy drugs to find. They can be found on propellants for whipped cream, in aerosol spray cans or room deodorants, freon, insecticides, hair spray and paints.

For adolescents, these are maybe the first substance used to get high. In many cases parents even buy them for use in shop at school, or even for daily use as hair sprays.

The use of inhalants produces an immediate high. It also has immediate negative effects such as nausea, sneezing, coughing, nosebleeds, fatigue, lack of coordination and loss of appetite. It can decrease the heart and respiratory rates. Long term use of inhalants may result in hepatitis or brain hemorrhage.

Inhalants have been called: laughing gas, whippets, poppers, snappers, rush, bolt, locker room, bullet, climax. If the use of inhalants is combined with other drugs it can cause unconsciousness, coma or death.

STIMULANTS

COCAINE

Cocaine is a drug extracted from the coca leaf. Cocaine stimulates the nervous system. It appears in many different forms. Normally it is a white crystalline powder, although sometimes it appears in big crystalline rocks called rocks. Ordinarily cocaine is inhaled or introduced to the nasal passages and then inhaled, some addicts inject it or smoke a form of the drug or freebase it.

Another form of the drug is the coca paste. This is the crude product smoked in South America. It can be especially dangerous since it contains other ingredients such as querosene which can damage the lungs.

The immediate effects of cocaine can be felt in a matter of minutes and reach a maximum high in an interval of 15 to 20 minutes. Some of the effects are: dilated pupils and elevated blood pressure, heart rate, respiratory rate, and body temperature.

The dangers of the use of cocaine vary according to the way it is administered, the dosage and the individual. Regular users declare depressed feelings, irritability, anxiety and insomnia, even a small doses of cocaine can cause psychological problems.

Chronic users can suffer from paranoia and it can create "Cocaine Psychosis". This state can cause tactile hallucinations. In occasional users it can cause a stuffy or runny nose, while in the chronic user it can ulcerate the mucous membrane. Injecting cocaine with unsterile utensils can cause AIDS, hepatitis and other diseases.

Yes, cocaine is a very dangerous drug and extremely addictive. Free basing can increase the risk for addiction. Free basing produces a shorter and more intense intoxication than any other way of using the drug. Since it is faster it also increases the risks associated with cocaine.

Cocaine is known by many names. Some of these are: coke, snow, flake, white blow, nose candy, big C, snowbirds, lady and many more.

Crack or Freebase rocks or rock is another type of cocaine. It is extremely addictive, and its effects are felt within 10 seconds. Crack looks like light brown or beige pellets and is often package in small vials and the user smokes it.

Cocaine kills by disrupting the brain's control of the heart and respiration.

DEPRESSANTS

Depressants decrease the functional ability of the user. In many ways its effects are similar to the effects of alcohol. As prescribed medically it can induce sleep and can be used as tranquilizers. In its abuse form it can cause slurred speech, staggering gait, and altered perceptions. In large doses it can cause respiratory depression, coma, and death.

The various types of depressant are: barbiturates, methaqualone, and tranquilizers. They are called downers, baros, blue devils, red devils, yellow jackets, Nembutal, Seconal, Quaaludes, Valium, Librium, Equanil, etc. They are normally in the form of tablets or capsules and are taken orally.

Chronic users of stimulants tend to use stimulants during the day and depressants at night. This can interfere with the normal physiology of the system and cause physical and mental illnesses.

NARCOTICS

These are derivatives of opium or synthetic substances. They can produce drowsiness, nausea, and vomiting. It can also produce constricted pupils, watery eyes, and itching.

Heroine is the narcotic most commonly abused. Its use is illegal in the United States. It is a white to dark powder and it has a variation called Black Tar which is a tar-like substance with a smell similar to vinegar. It is normally injected, although it can also be smoked or inhaled through the nasal passages.

Tolerance to narcotics develops rapidly and dependence is likely. Like other drugs that can be injected the user runs the risk of developing AIDS, hepatitis endocarditis and other infections.

Other types of narcotics are: methadone, codeine, morphine, meperidine, opium and others. Some of their names are: smack, horse, brown sugar, black tar, Empirin compound with codeine, codeine in cough medicines, pectoral syrup, Darvon, Talwin, Percocet, Paregoric and many more. It can be in the form of a liquid, capsules, tablets, and powder. It can be injected, inhaled through the nasal passages, smoked and taken orally.

HALLUCINOGENS

These are chemical substances extracted from plants or synthetic drugs. The two best know to the general public are PCP (Phencyclidine) and LSD (Lysergic Acid Diethylamide).

Because of the adverse effects of PCP, all production of this drug is presently done in clandestine laboratories. PCP interrupts the functions of the neocortex, that section of the brain that controls the intellect. Some of its effects are slowed time and body movements, dulling of the muscular coordination and senses and incoherent speech. Large doses may produce convulsions and coma, heart and lung failure, or ruptured blood vessels in the brain.

LSD known as Acid, comes from a mushroom that grows in some plants. A doses of LSD has been known to last for 8 to 16 hours. It causes illusions and hallucinations. LSD is known to have delayed effects, or flashbacks. The users of LSD experience panic, confusion, suspicion, anxiety and loss of control.

The types of hallucinogens are phencyclidine, lysergic acid diethylamide, mescaline and peyote, and psylocybin. Other names for them are: PCP, angel dust, loveboats, lovely, LSD, acid, green or red dragons, sugar cubes, mesc, buttons, magic mushrooms, mushroom, etc. They can come in pill, capsules, liquid, tablets, fresh or dried mushrooms, and gelatin. They can be taken orally, injected, smoked, chewed or licked off paper.

OTHER STIMULANTS

The chemical properties of stimulants accelerate the activity of the nervous system. They can cause increased heart and respiratory rates, elevated blood pressure, dilated pupils, and decreased appetite. Extreme use of stimulants can cause rapid or irregular heartbeats, tremors, and cause something users normally call a "rush".

Besides cocaines, other types of stimulants are Amphetamines, Methamphetamines and others such as, Ritalin, Didrex, Tepanil, etc. They are usually in the form of a pill, capsule or tablet. They can be taken orally, injected or inhaled through the nasal passages.

Some of the street names are: speed, uppers, ups, Black Beauties, Pep Pills, Crank, Crystal Methedrine, Crystal, Footballs, etc.

ABOUT THE AUTHOR

Gustavo Gil is a native Venezuelan. He played professional baseball from 1959 to 1976. He played winter ball for 19 years. Presently he coaches for the Yankee System in the Carolina League for the Prince William Yankees. Since 1977 he has been involved with the Yankee System as a coach at Fort Lauderdale, Florida State League; the West Haven Yankees, Eastern League; and as Manager, Danville, Midwest League. He also served as a Scouting Supervisor in Latin America for the California Angels in 1979.

Mr. Gil has worked as a television commentator on Major League "Game of the Week" broadcast to Caracas, Venezuela. He is founder and President of Gonzalo Marquez "Foundation for the Professional Player". He has received a degree in Sports Administration from Santa Maria University in 1987 and holds a broadcasting license from the Republic of Venezuela.

Mr. Gil, fondly called "el maestro" (the teacher) in Venezuela, conducted a series of Coaches Awareness Clinics throughout the nation sponsored by General Motors of Venezuela. These clinics where directed at coaches using the techniques described on his booklet and warning coaches on the signs of drug abuse by their players.

Printed in the United States
By Bookmasters

Printed in the United States
By Bookmasters